MRS. CARTER

SEDUCTION

7 golden rules

About me

Hi, I'm Natalia.

I am from Europe and currently live in Pompano Beach, Florida.

I did not think that someday I would be able to live wherever I wanted but the favorable circumstances and courage made my life look very interesting.

I am sorry for my English. This is not my native language. I lived in Europe for most years. I constantly improve my English. I also learn Spanish because I really like this culture. I can make some linguistic mistakes but the most important thing for me is to share my knowledge with you. You are consciously reading this book. You are looking for specific knowledge.

I will gladly share with you my rich experience.

What I do every day?

I work as a photomodel for the largest fashion houses around the world. I participate in advertising campaigns. It is funny, my career was to go in a completely different direction.

I graduated in law and obtained a master's degree in law. My parents wanted me to become a lawyer and I did not have the courage to act otherwise. It was only when I graduated that I saw that I was going the wrong way. I did not want to go the same way. This is not for me, I thought.

I've always been interested in modeling, I loved and love to pose for the camera.
I decided to start doing what I really like. And I started. It paid off.

My great appetite for the world and the desire to explore the secrets of men and women made today we meet in this book. I have also made many mistakes before this book was made. I used to have permanent problems with men. My life did not look like I wanted to. I was alone for a long time and it was more and more afflicting me.

Lonely days and nights. Everyday the same!
I only relied on myself. No support, no intimacy, no passion ... It killed me. I did not know where the problem is. I did not know why I only made fleeting acquaintances that did not interest me. I wanted to be in a strong relationship. I needed a partner, a lover and a friend.
I found.
These are my very personal confessions.

I could not write this book if I had not experienced a male / female failure. In fact, the biggest education for me were all my mistakes and failures. They taught me how to change a man's attitude and how to become a woman he

wants and wants to be with.

Why I wrote this book?

I always liked to help people. I know, however, that I will not do it only through my thoughts.

I want women who have the same problems to find an effective solution.

I want them to get a better understanding of themselves. Perhaps this book will encourage you to ask questions.

If you want to learn, the teacher will find you.

It's an honor for me to be able to share with you a few private thoughts on a hot topic that gives and will always give great emotions and blush.

I want to reach readers from around the world. I wrote this book to help many women understand the fundamental laws that apply between a woman and a man. This book is primarily for people who want to explore the secrets of seduction.

For a very long time I was going to comment on the subject of seduction in the book but I always postponed it until later the right moment came to share my thoughts with you.

Please remember once again that the language in which I write is not my native language and forgive me for any grammatical errors that may

arise. I strongly believe that my message will be received properly. I do not set any limits. I do not belong to people who go where everyone is.

I'm not interested in being a normal person.

I am most interested in you to benefit from me. The most important thing for me is to help you with matters that you reach for.

I know that you receive my sincere help that I bring for you in this book. I hope you will be happy to unpack the surprises that I have prepared for you here. Take a comfortable position and relax! You are getting closer!

The value here is dictated by experience. I want to change the bad beliefs people have for various reasons.

However, it is not easy to change your thinking. It is not enough to read a book without the contribution of your own work. Look carefully at all 7 rules that I have here. Think about them. Take as much as you can for yourself.

Many women have a blocked activity through their thinking. You are not such a woman. You are open, resourceful, sensual, energetic and hungry for knowledge. That's why you reached for this book. I'm going to give you a lot to think about and teach you what principles to follow.

I want you to get a full grip. Use your prescriptions readily. Try to always remember the most important things. Try to always think about the

key issues that are most important to you and your partner. Remember also that you treat yourself well. Always listen to your inner voice. He tells you well. Focus on the emotions you feel at the moment. Do not underestimate them. Correspond with them.

Seduction is a secret and subtle tool.

I am sorry if you expect a stroke and that after reading this book everything will do the same, well - it will not. Your work on yourself is key here.

My goal is to show you how you achieve what you want. But remember one! You can do nothing without your participation.

Be careful. Just like you, I am a woman. I know what language we use. I know how we operate and what expectations we have for men.

I am exploring this world because I have always been interested in this subject. Ever since I remember, I've always been interested in interpersonal relationships. As I began to become a woman, I was also interested in the world of men.

How do they work? What drives them? What do they think about and what they really want?

Many such questions circulated in my head.

It's nice to be in their world.

They think the same about us.

Do you want to learn more?

I am inviting you to the further part of my reflections.

Mrs. Carter

What I have prepared for you?

I prepared this book so that it would serve you. Use it wisely. I deeply believe that the greatest principles of seduction will be well absorbed by you and that you will successfully apply them in your life.

Live, guided by an attitude of positive expectations, knowing that everything that brings you life, somehow works in your favor. Remember that you always expect miracles because you yourself are a miracle.

Remember that if you feel you want to do something, do it now. The days that will come are numbered. Live life to the full as long as you live. Have fun, be crazy. Do not treat life with seriousness that deprives you of spontaneity and pleasure.

Think about changes in your life. They are the only and certain element of our life. Think about what can change for the better in your life. Speak to compliment yourself and others. Do not be afraid of it.

This will also affect you well. Use skills learned during this reading. You need to know what you want and the rules that you will find here, adjust to yourself.

Get ready! We are fast approaching the most important and strongest rules that are in seduction.

Get Ready!

1
Influence the signals your body sends

There are several tricks that women use consciously or not to get men's attention. They want to give them a signal that they are interested in making friends. In the same way, they want to let them know that they are ready to deepen relationships. Interestingly, these tricks are simple and effective.

We start by looking into the eyes. The man usually reads this as a signal to act. Thanks to this, he is sure that he will not be rejected. An additional plus is a moisturized mouth. It's very sensual. It is a promise of a kiss.

You can also gently touch the glass or spectacle frame with your finger. It is a very readable sexual signal. It is good that you touch your neck or shoulders. It's a message that you have a desire for a tender touch of a strong erotic stimulus. The man will imagine that he is touching you.

2
Let him fight

The most important thing is to let the man feel that he is a warrior.

He must feel that he has fought for you. It's not about pretending to be a princess locked in a tower. You must wake the spirit of the conqueror in the man. If something comes too easily to us - we do not value it. This is not attractive for us. It is worth to remember about it at every stage of acquaintance.

How to build a perfect relationship? Act like in dance. Take two steps forward and one step back. When you are at a meeting do not let it last for a very long time. Stop them when the emotions are still strong. If a man proposes another meeting, plan it in a few days. You must ensure that there is a feeling of insufficiency.

This greatly strengthens the tension and increases the willingness to further develop the situation. You will find that it will be the driving force of your relationship.

3

Ask for help
that you will
need it

What is the best way to start a new relationship? Ask for help or a small favor. This can be the beginning of a promising relationship. You never know what will happen later. Give him a chance to prove himself. Each man has a deeply rooted desire to help the weaker. Ask him to show you the way. Ask him to give you something that is heavy. It does not matter that you could deal with it yourself. Let him feel that he is needed. He must feel that he is needed.

At this moment the subconscious will also work. Looking after a woman is a traditional male role.

You, as a woman, will have the opportunity to express your gratitude. And there is no better aphrodisiac than admiration in the eyes of a woman. Do not trust? Admit that usually very independent women are lonely. I was such a woman myself for many years before I learned how to deal

with a man correctly.

4

Ask about things that are interesting to him

Once the knowledge has been made, prove to him that he really interests you. During the date, talk mainly about him. Ask him what he enjoys. What is his hobby? You do not need to know about motorization or football. All you have to do is ask and listen to the answer.

Thanks to this he will feel important and interesting. In his mind there will be an association: a feeling of pleasure caused by a conversation on a favorite subject and a person with whom he talks about it. What will be the effect?

The memory of that date will evoke those emotions that passion provides. There is, however, a very important benefit! The man does not forget the woman who showed him interest.

5

Agree to do something just for you

He must change his plans for you. He wants to go to Colombia? Let it wait until it suits you, or pour it together into a different place. Let it take you on a romantic trip to Italy, which you will remember for good.

Do you think it is binding? And very well! Agree without any resistance to smaller and bigger sacrifices. If you want, you can gently urge him to do some things. Give him reason to think about it. Give him reasons to be active. Let him give you a gift idea for your brother. Invite him to a corporate event.

The most important thing is that the man puts as much energy as possible into a relationship with a woman. The more energy he puts into his acquaintance with a woman, the more he will care about continuing this relationship. His involvement increases more if more effort is made. He will not be able to withdraw so easily.

You do not believe that it works? You probably know more than one pair, where she is like a princess and he is happy ...

6
Cooperate with him

People who feel good in their presence - unknowingly - take the same positions, imitate their movements, even adjust themselves with their breath.

Psychologists have proved that such a mechanism works perfectly in male-female relationships. Try to match your partner. If he leans in your direction, return it. Take a similar position, repeat his gestures. Remember! Keep neutrality! This is a very important issue. Speak with a similar tone of voice.

You will see that it will spark between you soon. Also make sure that you sit in front of him or on his right.

By doing so, you will use strong subconscious information! The people who sit on our right side are considered favorable and nice and good. We think so even when we do not know this person.

7

Think the best about yourself

This is the most important stage of our journey. What you think of yourself as a woman, how you feel in your own body, is the basis of how you act on men. Because of how you feel with yourself, men perceive you.

My friend was once in New York and while visiting the city, he noticed that it is full of extremely beautiful women. Most of them emanated with beauty and grace. He could not get over how many beauties were found in one place. He thought: Maybe it is thanks to plastic surgery? In the end, they are very popular here.

However, after some time he began to notice that not all of these women are beautiful, but that real attractiveness flows from inside them. The way they walked, moved, looked, made him perceive them as beauties. Later he had the opportunity to meet some of these women and it turned out that each of them had deeply positive beliefs about their own worth and beauty.

I do not know if you ever wondered what you are like?

What governs your behavior and what is important to you? How is it with this seduction in your life? Sometimes, one event makes you start to see yourself as a person with some feature.

It is rare that our ideas about ourselves are a real reflection of reality. And it does not matter if you believe that something is possible for you. All beliefs affect your behavior to varying degrees.

It is good to have good and supportive beliefs about yourself. I want you to think about yourself and what you think. Go inside yourself now.

I am asking you to do some exercise. What are your beliefs about yourself as a woman and your attractiveness? Write down thoughts that will come to your mind.

Exercise 1

Beliefs about the environment - men. Convictions about the seduction and attractiveness of other women:

Exercise 2

Beliefs about how you can seduce:

Exercise 3

Beliefs about what is important to you in seduction:

Exercise 4

Beliefs about how you are a woman:

42

Exercise 5

What is your mission:

Thank you. You have just done a lot on the path of your change. The time has come to make all positive beliefs become your beliefs forever.

Think about how much richer you will be thanks to your beliefs? Imagine yourself now how you act with these new beliefs. Imagine a few new situations. See how you talk freely with the man you are interested in. You look at him and you know that he can be faithful and affectionate. You see in his eyes a flash of fascination and you know that you are a woman with whom he wants to be.

Summary:

1. Pay attention to what you like in yourself.

2. Take care of your body.

3. Pay attention to what you wear.

4. Make yourself phenomenal.

5. Touch and flirt.

6. Seduce with your fragrance.

7. Do not limit yourself

A place for your notes

A place for your notes

A place for your notes

A place for your notes

A place for your notes

A place for your notes

A place for your notes

A place for your notes

A place for your notes

A place for your notes

A place for your notes

A place for your notes

A place for your notes

A place for your notes

A place for your notes

A place for your notes

A place for your notes

A place for your notes

A place for your notes

A place for your notes

A place for your notes

A place for your notes

A place for your notes

A place for your notes

A place for your notes

A place for your notes

A place for your notes

A place for your notes

A place for your notes

A place for your notes

A place for your notes

A place for your notes

A place for your notes

A place for your notes

A place for your notes

A place for your notes

A place for your notes

A place for your notes

A place for your notes

A place for your notes

A place for your notes

A place for your notes

A place for your notes

A place for your notes

A place for your notes

A place for your notes

A place for your notes

A place for your notes

A place for your notes

A place for your notes

A place for your notes

A place for your notes

A place for your notes

A place for your notes

A place for your notes

A place for your notes

A place for your notes